Gallery Books
Editor: Peter Fallon

THIRST

David Wheatley

THIRST

Gallery Books

Thirst
is first published
simultaneously in paperback
and in a clothbound edition
on 30 October 1997.

The Gallery Press
Loughcrew
Oldcastle
County Meath
Ireland

ISBN 1 85235 207 8 (*paperback*)
     1 85235 208 6 (*clothbound*)

The Gallery Press acknowledges the financial assistance
of An Chomhairle Ealaíon / The Arts Council, Ireland,
and the Arts Council of Northern Ireland.

Contents

for my parents

thirsting away, you don't know what for
                    — Beckett, *The Unnamable*

Sleepwalking

I want to feel it again: what I felt
when I woke once standing in the kitchen
after walking downstairs in my sleep.
The school bags had all been lined up
and the lunches packed in clingfilm
by the fridge, gurgling to itself,
but this was hardly the kitchen
of the evening before, the unusual shape
in the corner that was a brush then
could hardly be the brush that we used
for sweeping the tiles, and the goldfish
rubbing its nose on the glass of its bowl,
were I to hazard a finger, could
hardly but have developed a taste
for flesh, or so I thought.
I moved with the new-found awkwardness
of a woken sleepwalker across the floor
and towards the stairs and the more familiar
strangeness of dreams, but looked back
once to see it again: the kitchen
like a charcoal drawing, the table
set for my absence, this new place
I had seen for the first time
stripping of meaning the place that I knew
without a word or a struggle, threatening
only that it might become habitable.

Bray Head

A whisper of breeze parting the pubic gorse;
the startled scald crow leaves only its shadow.
Further off a ferry scabs the sea.
The taste of the gorse heavy in the air.
The one thing the fog over the mountain
lifts on this morning disturbing the scene

is me, tracing a line over the mountain
between the plain and twitching sea,
the sound of my footsteps troubling the air
as little as my figure alters the scene.
The single crow hanging over the gorse
covers my face with its shadow

and is gone as quickly towards the sea.
Ahead a summit beacon brands the air
where one rocky outcrop commands the scene.
Walking over the brow of the mountain,
I find myself trying to keep up with my shadow
steering ahead of me between the gorse.

I feel on the point of vanishing into the air:
I want to rise like the crow in the gorse,
sheer above its earthbound shadow
and silently as the thousand-feet-below sea,
dwindle to a tinier mark on the scene
than the footprints I leave on the mountain

and vanish unnoticed from the scene.
Shadows of clouds over the mountain
creep so far along the gorse
I hardly know the mountain from the shadow,
all perched between the plain and sea
like a landscape carved out of silence in air,

mountain, mountain path, the whole in shadow,
the fog a curtain lifted on the scene:
I making my way across the mountain,
the air so nearly alive with the smell of the gorse
and the ferry dark against the air,
somewhere the mountain meets the sky and sea.

The last fog-wisp lifts above the mountain.
One scald crow alighting in the gorse
is suddenly enough to complete the scene.

Fourteen

The skinned lab rabbit's blue cerebral lobes swimming in
  formaldehyde.

❖

Deliberately to wait to be lapped in the P.E. mile or not?
Slipping in with my chasers, I saw my own footsteps leave me
  for dead.

❖

French had an imperfect subjunctive, and nobody ever used it:
Serait-il possible que vous m'apportassiez un verre de vin?

❖

Could our French *assistant* but have grasped the pronunciation
of 'oink'.

❖

A Summer Project disco, an air guitar, and the dance floor all
  mine.

❖

My alarm increasing, as the year wore on, at Morrissey's
  bouffant —
Was I This Charming Man, Still Ill, sure, even, What
  Difference It Made?

❖

But at fourteen to start coming down, like a child, with
    underpants stains —
my 'Look, no hands' on my BMX the usual hypocrite's boast.

❖

And with that, a sense of ending all round: something under-
    neath it all
that makes you run the opposite way from the rest one day in
    P.E.,
the lab rabbit crept from its glass jar escaping across the back
    fields.

Spleen

after Baudelaire

I've more memories than if I were a thousand years old.

An enormous chest of drawers in whose stuffed hold
you found poems, law-suits, billets-doux, balance-sheets,
romances, locks of hair rolled up in receipts,
would hold less secrets than my sad brain.
It's a pyramid, an immense souterrain
sealing in more dead than a mass grave.
I'm a loathsome cemetery no moonbeams ever pave,
whose crawling worms — just like remorse — once released
will always choose the sweetest corpse on which to feast.
I'm an old boudoir that's been filled with faded roses,
sepia tableau a forgotten style composes
out of gloomy pastels and engravings, trailed
in perfume some unstoppered flask's exhaled.

There's nothing that can match these limping days for length,
when our boredom, ground down by the silent strength
of snowy years, dismal and incurious fruit,
learns to live in immortality's salute.
Henceforth, living matter, you are nothing more
than a granite rock encircled by vague terror
snoozing at the bottom of a Saharan mist;
an old sphinx world-forgotten and oblivion-kissed,
on no map, and whose foul humours sing for no one
now except the last rays of the dying sun.

A Paris Notebook

I SHAKESPEARE & CO

George drove his moped through the door one day
'to see if we were awake'. The upstairs shelves groaned
with first editions; the beds, or cots, to which we always
    preferred
the uncarpeted floor, were crawling with lice. Antlered Notre
    Dame
filled the window at night like a trophy-room moose in stone.
There was never enough to eat and always too much to drink.

Kingsmill, Hugh's son, shared a Greek island with Leonard
    Cohen
in winter but had to borrow money for breakfast. On the shop
stamp were the words 'Kilometre zero'. All roads started
    there.
And on the shopfront plaque, round Whitman's haggard
frontiersman features — *the* Whitman, not George — the
    words
Étranger qui passe tu ne sais pas avec quel désir je te regarde.

2 MÉTRO

Before the platform proper
of each station I'd see a
    lit tunnel leading nowhere,
but never be able to find it when
    I went looking. Stations
had novelists' names — Zola, Goncourt,
    Dumas — and lines
that meshed like plots I would never
    unravel; all the map
lacked was a Throw 6 to Start.
    I'd ride and ride
for the sake of it, watching other trains
    vanish down turnings
at junctions in bursts of St Elmo's fire, métro-
    style, from the points:
comings, goings. I was sixteen
    and piecing the city around me
together from scraps like these, stations whose
    names were enough to make me
get off and explore; Paris by numbers.

3 SECONDS, BEAUBOURG

The first thing I couldn't believe was how dirty it was,
though I may have suspected the dirt, too, was 'modern'.
Beaubourg was *toutes tripes dehors*, all its guts hanging out,
pumping its gobbled-up tourists along
the escalator for the view from the roof —
Hôtel de Ville, Sacré Cœur, Défense —
like one long crazed digestive tract.

Below in the square a clock was counting down
to the year 2000 in seconds,
four hundred million give or take,
with fruit-machine rolls to conjure its jackpot.
I set the time delay on my camera, stood back
from the ledge to wait and started to count:
10, 9, 8, 7, 6, 5, 4, 3, 2, 1 . . .

4 DEGAS AND THE ABSINTHE-DRINKER

Days when the world looks best
through the yellow-green, wormwood
filter of an absinthe glass
that smells of hyssop, fennel, aniseed;

afternoons that shade
into evenings unprotestingly;
evenings sleepily dragging on
till closing time . . .

Days when the only smile
you want to see is on your
own slow-parting lips reflected
in the glass you drink from —

I am there too and breathe
the same exhausted atmosphere,
sharing your drip-fed, sullen vacancy
and trying not to catch your eye.

My back to the wall in a corner
I sketch and make plans to fill
your glass with drink
enough for both of us one day,

on the canvas where —
the scene expressly posed
this time — I know our paths
will finally recross.

I picture it now, the serenity
of a drunken night
preserved in oils, made
proof against its dissolutions:

the empty bottle beside you
like a sanctuary lamp
glowing in permanently
mirrored bar-room light,

the expression on your face
as dry as its make-up
or the paint in which
I smudge it on a second time,

and I am shocked in advance
to think what little
effort such polychrome
despair need cost;

the thought of your glass,
your empty glass, overflowing
before your eyes forever
almost sobering somehow.

5 NOTHING TO DECLARE

My ears popped as the 737 cleared the tarmac,
unpopped again to the captain's *Céad Míle Fáilte* two miles up.

'Nothing to Declare' then: exchanging one Departure Lounge
for another as simply as I set my watch back an hour . . .

And reaching into my pocket in Dublin for busfare home
I found handfuls of marvellous, suddenly worthless coins.

Lithuania

A long, briny Baltic comber slaps against
the dyke, comes apart in hundreds-and-thousands

of froth all round you and soaks you through: *Effi Briest*
   weather.
The coal-eyed old Jew stares into a pointed camcorder

while a guanoed Lenin doffs his cap,
propped rigid in cast-iron, epochal sleep:

the very man, of all the kitsch-bazaar *matryoshka*
dolls on show to shade the competition by a whisker —

not forgetting Stalin inside with his cowlick, Brezhnev
   with his scowl.
Each gravid doll's a Jonah and a whale

at once: you buy one, take a snap of the crocus-bulb church
spilling pushy mass-goers out of its narrow porch

while you're at it, shawls, greatcoats whipped up round them
in the wind; buy a hat as well; and all it takes is a random

cloudbreak parting the damp air round you like a sword
for the scene to be pinned to memory like a postcard.

A Skimming Stone, Lough Bray

for Justin Quinn

Skim a stone
across the lake surface,
marrying water and air:
turn this brick
of earth, while it flies,
from stone to living fire.

From stone to living
fire ablaze
on the lake's faceted skin —
tideless, the plaything
of wind and rain,
as now of this skimmed stone.

Watch the stone brush
the water beneath it
and never fall below,
dip for an instant,
rise again
and glide like so, like so.

Hear it echo back
each new contact,
brushing against the surface,
like a whip cracked
from shore to shore
of this walled-in, echoing place.

Skim a stone
across the lake surface,
never suspect it may fall —
as long as there's water
left to walk on,
air for its echo to fill.

Littoral

Municipal statues outside
the water-treatment works,
gulls swooping round the outflow pipes,

thrashing dogfish the pier-end anglers
leave to die; a beer-glass on a car bonnet
and the bladderwrack rancid in the heat;

the off-white pellets of the ammonia train
coming singing round the Head
and the neat green mantis

of the suburban electric prodding
out of the tunnel on the other side of the bay . . .
The sun plays with the goose-pimpling botch

of pink and white that is the flesh's
first coy greeting to the summer.
One afternoon of it and you're both

old hands again: look, just look at you
scanning the dunes for a quiet spot
to scatter the months in since your last time

like the fine dry sand you bend
to scoop from the rock-pool in the cove
and let slip through your fingers . . .

Verlaine Dying

for Sinéad Morrissey

It is my last winter, and all
the dying I have done with now
was for nothing, if not to hear
a thrush part the air above
the woods where we walked

and know that I, as much
as anyone, have only ever
half believed such things.

Giacometti, c. 1952

It is the clamped jaw
and boxer's hands that catch the eye

in the photograph, the index finger
pointing towards the ground;

the taste for perfection on speaking terms
with the dripping basement studio

and endless scruffy shirts. The figures,
Genet wrote, were offerings

to the dead, and death was gravity:
the wire-supported hands dimpled

the air like mayflies' legs on water
in their tiny miracle of balance.

Up they grew like rope tricks, the legs
left unattached and matchbox

Easter Island heads, the standing figures
and the figures striding nowhere

that were always where they had to be,
and as if already there forever

with their huge feet and the few square inches
of the bases that could be Archimedes'

one firm spot; there, in another
photograph, a whole roomful of them

and just the artist's head grinning
in a corner, wondering maybe whether

the best thing mightn't be to destroy
the whole lot now or work all night.

AM Radio

The static
is the sound of the world's
axis turning
as I finger the dial,

a chaos of voices
gasping for breath,
the short wave snoring
its dreams in white noise.

After-hours radio.
There is nothing to stay
awake for and nothing
to make me drift off.

Punctual, various
headlines leap time zones,
pips mark the hours
like morse ultimata;

one phone-in show host
keeps punting the dull
sludge of insomniac
chatter *ad nauseam*.

Sleep is beyond me:
each shake of my head —
half defiance,
half resignation —

stays creased in the pillow
I roll on. This smooth plastic
box devours sleep,
spits dreams out

and builds invisibly,
wide and high
as the room's four walls,
its babel in air.

And at odd moments,
unlooked-for, silence
descends between stations . . .
And it is as much

as my ear can do
to tell the radio's
tiny silence
from that of the night.

Bedsits

What the breeze
in the rickety casements
is really doing —
it makes sense

as well — is eavesdropping
on the patchwork
of windows where
coffee-fuelled talk

goes on
under sixty-watt
bulbs well
into the night

and drifts
to sleep among
easy rituals —
a snatch of a song;

a gulped
sleeping pill;
milk cartons left
on the ledge; an angle-

poise lamp nodding
off in a window;
invisible hands
drawing the curtains to.

Litter

It could be a chip bag
thrown from a car window
or a page from the evening football edition
I'm watching blow down the road
this Saturday night,
get caught in the wheels
of the hurrying traffic,
and flap like a squashed, giant
origami gull.

Nothing belongs to a street
like litter, nothing is truer
to every last crack in the pavement,
the gutters and drains
we hardly notice,
than the crisp bags and cigarette butts
that the rain dissolves
or the sweeper collects,
but that always come back;

and it is our sentimental
cleanliness that is transient,
the litter what will endure
of our streets:
a past that is always
with us and already
outliving the present,
yesterday's news
good enough for any tomorrow.

Illumination

'And did you know,' I asked her as we walked down
Aungier Street, 'that Saint Valentine's remains are kept in
a casket in' — pointing to it — 'Whitefriars Church?'
This was true, providing one did not make too much of
there being two versions of the historical Valentine. One
would have him a young Roman physician, the other the
elderly bishop of Terni; the two may even have been the
same person. Whatever the truth, today was his feastday
and we slunk inside, glad of the excuse to be out of the
rain. Whitefriars is one of those happy places, increas-
ingly rare even in Dublin, into which the light of day
seems never to penetrate. The sum effect was a wholly
salubrious gloom, only relieved by a few guttering
candles here and there and the far-off sanctuary lamp. We
made our way to the casket and hunkered down to inspect
it. Lost in contemplation, I found three images from
memory swimming in front of my eyes. The first was a
Valentine card I had been tempted to buy the previous
day, with a battery-operated *I Love You* that lit up when
it was opened. I spent several minutes experimenting with
it, as with a fridge door, looking for the exact moment
when the light came on, but in the end decided against it.
The second was Rudolph Valentino in *The Four Horse-
men of the Apocalypse*, which we had spent a long after-
noon over the previous Christmas watching on Channel
4, enjoying in particular the celebrated tango scene,
which we spent a half-hour later that evening trying to
recreate. The third was a memory of a long-dead school-
friend whose middle name I saw initialised once on an
attendance form as 'V'; when I asked what it stood for he
told me it was Valentine. He didn't like people knowing
about it, fearing our adolescent ridicule, and the first that
most of us heard of it was when it was too late even for
that, at his funeral. He had died, I should say, of a sudden
liver infection. What I remember most vividly about him

now is his curly brown hair.

I was happy to see the rain had eased off outside. The thought of hair reminded me that I could do with a shave. We walked down George's Street, past Thomas Moore's birthplace, Walton's, Bewley's, the Globe, and Castle House where my friend Dennis who worked in Customs and Excise was even then most likely hunched over his desk 'running the country' as he called it. Unlike mine, which came and went with a straggling unpredictability, his beard was a model of tonsorial good sense and purposefulness. Despite my misgivings about it I only ever asked for my beard to be trimmed, never shaved off entirely. Perhaps I preferred the cover the hair provided, just as I preferred the murk of the church to the daylight outside. I think this must have had something to do with it, since when I came out of the barber's I was stopped in my tracks with envy by the sight of the longest beard I'd ever seen on the face of a man emerging from the door of the Universal Hair and Scalp Clinic a few yards down the lane. What made it all the more striking was that, apart from the beard, I don't think he had a single hair on his head. On a whim my eyes glanced upwards at the clinic's antiquated neon sign, turned off as usual, which consisted of a male face arrested in an expression of ectoplasmic surprise, perhaps at the knowledge that the legend *Why Go Bald* had appeared in enormous letters under his head, or just, like me, biding his time for some more ordinary illumination that had not, as yet, occurred.

Landscape with Satellite Dish

Nothing ever seemed to happen in Springfield;
there was never anything good on TV.
Then the newsflash came through about the bomb.
Lisa stopped trying to electrocute Bart
to watch. 'Looks like we're in deep doo-doo,'
said Homer, going to fix himself a snack.

The hairs stood up on the back of Grampa's neck —
all thirteen of them. Who would save Springfield?
There was nothing anyone could do
except sit and keep watching TV.
By the fourth ad-break Homer was bored.
Who cared anyway about some stupid bomb?

'Didn't Professor Frink make a bomb-
defusing robot?' asked Bart. Yes, but there was a snag:
it kept blowing up. A tearful Marge bared
her soul to the cowering shoppers of Springfield —
'We could lose everything, even TV' —
and hid the family savings in her hairdo.

Then Homer had an idea, chewing his do-
nut — let Mr Burns take care of the bomb.
That weirdo! He didn't even have a TV.
Homer got on the phone to Burns, snug
in his fallout shelter, and hollered: 'Save Springfield!'
Now he was thirsty, and headed off for a beer

at Moe's. Jasper was crying into his beard
at the bar: soon he'd be as dead as a dodo
and nothing would remain of dear old Springfield
but roaches and fallout, all because of the bomb
some two-bit punk was using to cock a snook
at folk like him and get some time on TV.

Burns was on the job though. Of course he watched TV;
he'd staged the whole thing to help him sweep the board
at the Oscars with his new film *Sneak
Attack*, a Wellesian thriller. 'Think of the dough
I'm going to make,' he chortled to Smithers. The bomb
was a hoax — what a lucky escape for Springfield!

TV announced the news to the people of Springfield.
Bored again, Homer forgot all about the bomb
and sneaked to the fridge for a beer. It was empty. Doh!

Weekend Driving

Cresting the hill, slipping the clutch,
I find a lay-by to pull into,
deserted this Sunday evening, from which
to look down on the rain-drenched view.

Mosaic of fields and ditches veined
with here and there a road, stray cars,
a driver's light brooding behind
intermittent windscreen wipers.

Behind me the bend in the road I'll take
to exchange this valley for another,
and more turns off the beaten track
I'll follow to end up wherever.

No sign the rain is going to let up,
no urgent reason for going on.
I release the brake and go over the top,
incorrigible, putting my foot down.

The Accident

Misjudging the turn and going too fast at thirty
to hold the road, I've time to size up the doom-
pregnant vignette — the wintry ditches abruptly

foreclosing the mountains, the jaunty holly in bloom —
before the two or three seconds that are all
that it takes and the car exchanges the road for the ditch,

bumping my head on the roof but breaking nothing,
the stereo keeping going with scarcely a hitch . . .
We're stuck fast. I'm about to walk to the nearest

house when three men in a Range Rover pull
round the corner, stop and get out. 'Need any help?'
We spit on our hands, push, and manage to get the thing

free to a self-congratulatory yelp.
The men disappear, trailing our thanks. I dust
my clothes down; we get back in. All this has taken

roughly five minutes. I hazard a joke, you laugh;
we drive away, the ice we skidded on broken —
some girls on the road behind us waving us off.

In Glencullen

A broken mirror in a magpie's nest:
the jewel-thief coveting his very eyes.

❖

Beer-can piled on beer-can
by the fairy fort: a god is born.

❖

Pond scum stinking in the heat,
dragonflies flesh-wounds in the air.

❖

A skein of telephone lines winds
around the hillside fields: golf balls
soar above the links like grapeshot.

❖

Songs without words:
the pigeon on the gate,
the old grey goose,
the spring well,
the rocky road to Dublin.

❖

A Cheviot ewe licking afterbirth.
Soft to the touch, wool on a barbed-wire fence.

❖

A derelict lead mine's sultry
dry-stone chimney walls:
the heart of the world
long since gone up in smoke.

Alba

The river stuttering over its weirs to the bay
a heron sleeping erect in the shallows
a hook-necked swan treading the grey-black ferment of the tide
the pronged moon and a few weak stars overhead
and the papers in bundles outside shops and the shutters going
   up —

It's getting light. Light on the water and light in the streets:
an ecliptic sliver of gold along the cathedral's
cupola, the raindrops on the hedgerow leaves
seeded with light like amphibians' eyes.
The first train's whistle carries half-choked on the wind
from the station I'm walking towards and will reach
in good time to sit and watch the commuters descend on,
briefcases in hand and clutching their papers like scrolls,
from a second-class carriage. I'm running ahead of time
on nameless streets, an unopened umbrella
crooked on my arm or cheekily dragged along railings,
an aimless wire-haired mongrel jog-trotting
for a few hundred yards beside me, tail in the air,
then turning back as unpredictably as it arrived.

It's getting light. I look for the moment of secret convergence
of colour and blackness before day prevails,
the exact shade of its motionless doubt before birth,
like knowing a face and not being able
to give it a name, like catching a breath,
like the sound of a hesitation between 'yes' and 'no'.
I watch the deckle-edged skyline fade up
to all I remember, and match a vague mood of desire
to what I can only imagine the city containing:
raindrops shaken from the hedgerows falling
over your face and into my hand on your face
in a garden where birds peck at the winter earth
and find nothing, and a cat in the flower-bed arches

its spine to leap and stays put, a heron standing
on one leg under a beech tree in full
November disarray, curtains flapping loose
in an open window while I run barefoot over the lawn,
my fingers covered in earth; all in daydream;
and however I try to connect the water I hear
running in mains-pipes under the streets
with the raindrops that I imagine
falling over your face and into my hand
I fail.

      I tell myself it will have got light
in the pupils of your opening eyes, but in
your irises there is always room for sleep.
The dreams we will rise from tomorrow have started already,
threading their clew through labyrinths with no more
possible end than there is an end to the wrong turns
open to me whether I stay or go any further.
You too think you are free and move in a maze
however you try to believe the paths that led
you here were of your own choosing, or that you
are rooted any more deeply than the shadows
that climbed your bedroom wall as you slept.
There is only the dark and the light coming on.
Cats sit on doorsteps and wait to be fed; the newspapers
wait to keep their appointments over breakfast
with eyes still dull from the sleep they will hardly dislodge
and this is the day —

the hiss of a cigarette butt dropped in a platform puddle
newsprint on my fingers numb with the chill
coffee the colour of rust in a styrofoam cup
the sound of the leaving train's whistle
and under it the wind
that sooner or later will have to blow over.

The Heron

after Somhairle Mac Gill-Eain

A caustic yellow moon hemming the skyline,
unbroken earth never relaxing into
growth, the frozen air looking down
on waves where gold light has conjured a window.

The flimsy loveliness of the moon is not
the element my spirit bathes in tonight,
any more than the sea so coldly ornate
or the sound and fury of the breaking tide.

> *A strength its own martyr,*
> *death under my skin,*
> *the heart turned deserter,*
> *nothing to believe in.*

A heron dropped to earth with lowered eyes
stood erect among the wrack and weed,
both wings folded to her sides, and mistress
in her stare of all that she surveyed.

As helplessly alone beside the sea
as Newton's beachcomber seen from the further
shore, her brooding vigil probing for prey —
familiar hunger inviting familiar murder.

The mind woken to itself in unrest,
the curious flesh to the memory of its compulsion,
a sleepless disease no gleam of light has pierced:
music, delirium, revulsion.

It is the moment of frenzy that vouchsafes the light
to the blindly self-occluded brain,
the horizon breaking open at the thought
of a clearance smiling the darkness aside like a frown.

Observing the slippery calm of the bay
from the rough cobbles of the shore,
listening to the heaving brine spray
the rocks and the sea's suck and roar.

Left to herself, alone in creation,
however many her distant, invisible kin,
the bluely shining god's annunciation
bursts upon her while all around grows dim.

I am beside you and remain alone,
my watcher's eye as cold as the uncreased strait,
my ear cocked to the kiss of water on stone
bare flagstones on the littoral celebrate.

What is my thought any more than hers,
granted the beauty of the moon or sea:
vain daylight food or night's remorse,
dreamer's secret rose or poison tree?

The vision of a force that's loosed upon
the world released from doubt and sorrow's bind
like a vengeance, come its proper season,
is the only law to all her kind.

My vision too I have prised from all reproach,
broken, awry, temptation's-tinsel-tried,
wounded, waned, bleary-eyed and boorish;
brain, heart, love all grown unquiet.

At a Yüan Play

The Soul of Ch'ien-nü Leaves Her Body

Ch'ien-nü,
since she bade her betrothed, Wang Wên-Chü, farewell,
    has had no peace,
    and marks the emerald stalks
    in the bamboo grove
to count the days until he returns to her.

No Chang girl
for three generations has been married to
    a man not in
    the Imperial service;
    her love has travelled
ten thousand miles in search of an appointment.

Long before
his return — she fears from her dreams — he will have
    broken their vows.
    Now he writes to her mother
    confirming those fears:
he's coming home, and bringing 'the young mistress'.

Faithlessness!
Picture for yourself then the girl's reaction
    when, returning
    from the capital, her love
    brings with him on his arm,
his unfailing companion of three years —

Ch'ien-nü's
soul, her walking double (stolen away
from her body to be
with him all this time), come
to rejoin her, their
two loves twice as strong now in a single form.

A Garden in September

Inch by inch the oblong slab of sunlight
wins over the lawn;

we shift the wooden bench hourly
to stay in the shade

and watch the cardinal purple of tangling hebe
and wide-open clematis embroider

the far wall, where ants scramble
and leaves cover snails

spared the attentions of midday.
I have only to spill a glass of water

for the sun to lap it up at my feet.
But summer is ending,

and for more than the worm
the blackbird twitches impatiently

before swallowing. The tarmac
that baked so long in the heat has burst

to reveal a clump of underground mushrooms
already dead and beginning to stink,

and tomorrow something will be
not quite the same as we found it today

but still cause for neither regret nor alarm:
the chalked hopscotch grid in the lane

beginning to fade, the cat on the wall
picking its way more cautiously

through the scattered mosaic of jagged glass.

A Cold Snap

The sheep jostle to drink from the trough and shiver,
their dung in pellets dries into the soil.
The summer fires burnt the gorse right off.
The turn in the weather was due: the windmill on
the hillside reaps the whirlwind like so much largesse.

Best Man

for my brother

The rings in my pocket, the car in the drive ticking over . . .
I've watched you grow from boy into man and now
    bridegroom —
my senior in this, though four years younger than I am —
in tails and cravat as you finally answer the call

of a world of second cousins and half-great-uncles
who must suspect for all their mannerly pacts
(sandwich makers, carriage clocks)
that weddings and funerals are all that bind us together
now, if there was ever anything else . . .

Fidgeting with my cufflinks after the meal
and undecided on what I'm going to say
I joke with my mother, the suit I stand up in
to lift a glass in praise of permanent things
due back at the outfitter's the following day.

Lying in Late

Is there a history of wasted time?
Lying in late in a sweaty T-shirt and boxer
shorts I think I'm it, not moving a whisker.
The sheets around me are tossed like the scene of a crime.

A jacket I've draped on a chair is shrugging one shoulder.
There's no saying now what use the hours I've lost track
of could have been put to, or how to fill the remainder
till night; the one urgent thing is an itch in my back.

It strikes me again that the pillow has one head too few.
My eyes shut, I daydream another. The other is you:
you last till I blink, but leave the print of your head,

I'm convinced, on the linen, and with it a strand of your hai
A deserted house I could live with, but one deserted
by you . . . Old haunter, come clean: is that you not there?

Simone Weil in London

Prefer the absence of God to the presence of anything
else. I look to the sky for an answer and find one
of our own making; the bombs and flares
give off enough light, eerie-calm in its way,
to read or work by rather than sleep if I choose.

I eat no more than the prisoners do in the camps
but it is the truth that goes hungry, not this flesh
I let wither rather than glut with a lie,

and I feel it less real already, the breath in my mouth
that comes between me and the words that I pray,
my heartbeat that is enough to drown out His answer,
who does not answer, and it is a mercy

that nothing be left, not even belief, but prayer;
I make of my unbelief a kind of prayer.

Seven from Chamfort

La plus perdue de toutes les journées est celle où l'on n'a pas ri.

> count no day lost
> a laugh has cursed

❖

Ce que j'ai appris, je ne le sais plus. Le peu que je sais encore, je l'ai deviné.

> all once known now lost unmourned
> bar what remains to be unlearned

❖

L'Écriture a dit que le commencement de la sagesse était la crainte de Dieu; moi, je vois que c'est la crainte des hommes.

> Fear God, keep his laws and so be wise,
> avoiding those in whom his power lies.

❖

Il y a des redites pour l'oreille et pour l'esprit; il n'y en a point pour le coeur.

> Deaf ear, you've a second take;
> hearts you're on a single break.

❖

L'enfer: 'l'endroit où il pue et où l'on n'aime point'.

> hell reek
> like home
> all love
> clean gone

❖

*Seule l'inutilité du premier déluge empêche Dieu d'en envoyer
un second.*

> Only how little effect the first one had
> can have prevented God from repeating the flood.

❖

En voyant les hommes il faut que le coeur se brise ou se bronze.

> heart that sees
> break or freeze

Visiting Hour

Puce, there is no other word
for the colour of the upstairs ward
I find you in behind a curtain,
the sheets around your chin and smarting
from the elegant needlework
you've been stitched up with, still too weak
to raise a drip-fed arm to hold
the flowers I've brought in from the cold.

Oxygen masks above their heads,
the women in the next two beds
are swapping family histories
like symptoms of a shared disease:
the son one hopes will settle down,
the daughter in London, getting on,
another who works too hard to take
the time to visit. Maybe next week . . .

Even for the dying time
to kill is at a premium
in a place like this, its leaden dance
conducted by the ward clock's hands
forever stuck an hour before meals —
even when dinner consists of pills —
or programmes hardly up to much
they'll wheel you from the ward to watch.

The contours of your supine frame
beneath the sheets alone can tame
my fears that, shock-haired, wild and grim —
a Cheshire cat without the grin —
your cradled head is all that's left
of the failing body that I loved
and placed in a stranger's hands to cure
of sickness at its very core.

Now excised. Taking your wrist
I feel your dogged pulse protest
its unconcern and stake its claim
to the slow reflux of health again
through startled limbs, however scarred,
whatever you may have endured
carrying on as blithely as
the hair on a corpse's head still grows.

Surprised or not to be alive
you find you cannot help but thrive
on daily gifts of grapes and roses,
life in homeopathic doses:
an upturned, half-read paperback,
birds in the trees, their weak attack
of song at dawn, your morning glass
of barley water the colour of pus.

Under it all the unspoken trust
you merit more than self-disgust:
the prospect of being able soon
to dress, wash, feed yourself alone —
regain, if not *élan vital*,
sufficient recklessness of will
to trade your place here for a bed
in the larger, roofless ward outside.

A loud goodbye from another room.
Your eyes have closed. I'm needed at home:
I let our fingers disentwine,
moisten your dry lips with mine
and stand uncertain how to leave,
embarrassed at myself, relieved
by a nurse's head around the door
calling time on visiting hour.

Along a Cliff

for Caitríona O'Reilly

To start with there is the shell of a castle that rises
out of the foreland and over
the water we hear beneath us
standing inside its bare high walls.
On the far side of the castle are steps
cut into the rock that if you count them
make twelve going down, but, it's said,
thirteen when you come up, the extra step
like a piece of mythical flotsam
from a sea that has cast up Vikings,
St Patrick, almost the French, in its time.
We stand over it now like the latest in line.

I let you lead me along the low cliff edge.
On one side the drop to the water, on the other
flags on the green where golfers' strokes
thresh the air and send flying
coloured plastic tees we find in our path.
On one side the squeak of golf bags
being dragged away to the next hole,
on the other still the sound of the tide's endless churning
under arches and in invisible caves.

Anyone looking from a distance would see us
go missing and reappear among the grass banks
from moment to moment, like moles.
The beached seaweed is acrid and varicose.
A shallow rockpool brims to a thin algal soup
that a drowned bluebottle floats in, belly up.
Great worms of pipes and tubing
heave to the surface and rid themselves
of the leavings of earth in a slobbering wash
we pick our way through in unsuitable shoes,

straying lower over the rocks, closer
all the time to the diagonal line
of the sea on the shingle
until in the end we leave the rocks
and the scutch grass behind
to stand at its edge and survey
the long curve of the shore we have followed
and pick out the landmarks again
in an arc as wide as the whole field of our vision.

The wandering eye seeks out a focal point, but the bay
behind us looks flattened and drained of perspective,
absorbed into a texture of distance blending it
with the horizon. A raised thumb blots out
the castle that was so huge an hour ago
and dwarfs the golfers and flags on the green,
as detail by detail our gaze works further back
towards where we are standing
in search of some one thing to detach
from the rest and remember this by:
a child running towards us carrying a starfish,
the muddy pebbles small as birds' eggs
under our feet that the incoming tide
will have washed clean before it withdraws.

Wicklow, 1996

A Russian Notebook

after Mandelstam

What I say is just a rough draft —
whispered, since it isn't time yet.
Only heaven lifts the trophy, whose heft
of victory is all our blood and sweat.

And under purgatory's provisional sky
to have grown forgetful's not so rare —
not seeing that heaven's in our custody already —
the lifelong home we've carried with us everywhere.

2 THE GOLDEN GROVE

after Esenin

The golden grove has talked itself out
of the beech trees' happy language it once knew;
the dismal cranes show no more regret
for any of us below on their flights through.

What's to regret? We're all strangers here:
pass by, look in and leave the house again.
The hemp-fields' dreams, the full moon's over
the pond, are only of those that have passed on.

The bare plain falls away on every side
from where I stand alone, each wind-borne crane
dragged into distance. The happy youth I had!
Thoughts swarming on thoughts: regrets though, none

for any of the vainly squandered years
or for the lilac blossom of the soul.
In the garden somebody's lit fires
of rowan branches, but the flames blow cold.

The rowan bunches will not scorch;
this grass won't sere or shrivel. As the tree
sheds leaves softly from their summer perch,
I slough, and send my sad words on their way . . .

And if time, once they've been scattered to
the breeze, should rake them up again, saved
for a vain heap, just say the golden grove no
longer speaks the language I once loved.

Duet in Grey

I notice another grey hair tonight poking
through the brown. To it I say: welcome —
I hope you've invited the rest of your friends along.
No sign of baldness yet? All in good time,
but I can't devote myself to my hair non-stop.
Ageing means equal attention to every part.
Wrinkles, deafness, cataracts, penile droop
don't happen all by themselves: ageing means effort,
a clutching, rictal habit slowly spread
from ear to ear. Fail to die in your prime
and it's a life's work. Bedding down by your side
I'm heartened to see you too cultivating grey hair.
Could I be draining your colour, or you draining mine?
We clamber on top of and light our own funeral pyre.

Thirst

From this the poem springs: that we live in a place
That is not our own . . .
                    — Wallace Stevens

1

Ochre brown flashing copper and gold
as midday scintillates the Powder Tower
in which a crazed King Rudolf's magi toiled
with less success to transmute dross to ore —
a peripatetic Irishman, Ned Kelley,
among them. Now that I'm another one
I name him my precursor and my ally
in my search for the philosopher's stone.

2

A wall of tower blocks' Lubyanka eyes
blinks questions at me first thing every morning
(name, age, place of birth, political views)
as I down my cornflakes, shaved and yawning.
When I go to the window nothing seems to stir,
only a woman I think I glimpse now and then
avoiding my gaze and telling whoever's there:
'Occasionally I think I see a man.'

3

Occasionally in the garden I manage to catch
a bee in the act, exploring a buttercup
to carry off any nectar it can poach.
Each flower in sight's a future honeydrop
and as for the one I plucked all's not lost:
let's try the childhood game in which you hold
it to your chin and, if you're lucky, cast
a reflection the colour of butter, the colour of gold.

4

An abandoned Škoda, yellow paint peeling off.
Graffiti that look like unplayable Scrabble draws.
Dies caniculares: two dogs sniff
each other's arses, one starts licking its balls,
and a youthful striker's solitary ardour
pounds a gable end with kick after kick
but can't put even one away: the harder
he hits, the harder it comes pounding back.

5

No sooner do I board a tram than I'm smitten
with love for a dowdy beauty's Slavic nose
(Women of Prague!), then overcome with sudden
compassion for a *babička*'s scabby knees.
I watch her yawn, her mouth a huge expanse
of slobbering tongue, gap-teeth and fillings not
so bright that they eclipse or recompense
her for, beneath them all, a lifetime's rot.

6

Finery, finery . . . I ponder the Child of Prague,
orb in hand, crowned and robed in ermine,
presiding over a sneakered, bussed-in flock,
one of whom takes a snap and brings down a sermon
like a last judgment on his head from a monk.
I ponder how sacred and profane co-exist
in closer proximity than he cares to think:
Shake'n'snow Child of Prague, body of Christ . . .

7

Eight beatitudes arrayed between
the windows of the church's airy tambours
so far up the dome they can't be seen.
Not by me; to my weak eyes they're blurs
that signpost Palko's heaven like a threshold
I can't cross but only blankly stare at,
earthbound like the lowly wretch spreadeagled
under St Cyril of Alexandria's foot.

8

It's tedious, Cyril-Shmyril, your pose of spoilsport
Counter-Reformation hired muscle.
Since when has sainthood been a martial art?
Why not do something constructive, like write an epistle?
Start with one to the makers of Kafka T-shirts.
You could sign it 'Yours in pontifical goyness'.
Then a sterner one, to exchange-rate sharks.
But sternest of all: to bars that don't serve Guinness.

9

Dead July heat: the city imposes thirst
like a residence tax; the air constricts and claws,
diesel-heavy; the noon sun, doing its worst,
dissolves the traffic to a viscid haze
we follow the belltower stairs to try and climb
above, emerging to a view of hills
that comes like a suddenly remembered dream:
escape . . . The hour strikes with a peal of bells.

10

A mill in a wood in a valley: we get there at night,
kick off our shoes in a dark, enormous hall,
then follow the banister upstairs towards the light
where places at table will somehow be found for us all
and I, a total stranger, be invited
by the miller himself to drink my fill
before I tumble to sleep downstairs serenaded
by the river slowly turning the mill-wheel.

11

Take this ceremonial smack of a spoon
against an oil-lamp for a tuning fork
and tell me what key the birds are singing in
as evening rallentandos towards the dark.
Strain and you can hear the bat's falsetto,
the snake's elusive shuffle in the grass.
Listen: even the bloodsucking mosquito
with its single note is droning sonatas.

12

I love Scarlatti's grace notes like plucked strings,
Haydn's practical jokes in a powdered wig,
and how uproariously Debussy swanks
in preludes like the one for Mister Pickwick;
I love as well how this old piano disguises
my mistakes with its pedal's hollow boom,
and how the fade-out after playing teases:
'Find a better way to fill the room.'

13

I'm going to kill that mosquito: it makes me sick
being woken by its parasite caress
to find its sweet-tooth sinking in my neck,
and how it could suck me dry for all it cares;
my skin's like a relief map with its bites.
My very poems rail at the abuse:
my fountain pen keeps spluttering, then writes,
'Your blood belongs to no one else but us.'

14

An ignorant cityman who's never known
the names of plants in English, never mind Czech,
I find myself stopped short by the tell-tale sign
of blushing red in the grass beside the track:
strawberries I stoop to eat in handfuls,
strange to the taste, dissolving sweet-severe
to leave me red-faced at my greedy impulse,
wet-lipped, sticky-fingered like a lover.

15

Every walk we take in the wood circles
back to this one place we can't keep away from,
a wall of rock that rises from nowhere and curls
in on itself, the perfect mountain cwm.
And best of all, with an echo. As we get near
you shout ahead in a speculative tremolo:
I step forward just in time to hear
it fade away on a last unanswered 'hello'.

16

City, city, your distant tarmacked heart
calls weekenders home in speeding hatchbacks,
impatient for another week to start.
The car slips into the traffic and attacks
the kilometre-count on sudden road signs
looming out of the dark along our route
past small-town cafés, farmhouses down lanes
where the last of Sunday evening is played out.

17

Out of the world of July sunsets draped
like golden peacocks' tails across the river,
glinting from infinite eyes or lazily flapped
in the wind and shaking colour everywhere,
I try slowing down to a moment of pure stasis
the action of light on water, its flickering dance
too quick for my eyes; dizzy, they trump Heraclitus
on flux: failing to enter the same river once.

18

One brush with the weir is enough, its liquid scream,
and the meniscus of calm has come unstuck,
bundling the river on its way downstream.
Illusion of stillness, there is no winning you back:
the glass harmonica player on the bridge
has only to run his finger over its rim
for the smallest wine glass to get the itch
and overflow with a minute, ghostly hum.

19
Dusk, the Letná metronome blunt
against the sky: the music is over. The street's
a pool of shadows I've begun to blend
into when past me in the darkness flits
that impudent wretch Ned Kelley, shorn of his ears,
his crystal ball abandoned by its ghosts
and he, a ghost himself, to the gibes and leers
of the Castle gargoyles leaning from their roosts.

20
There was no philosopher's stone. Kelley, old crook,
your final occult brew — the only one
to work — was the suicide draught you took
in prison, broken, desperate and alone.
This last drink tonight's for you then, friend:
moonlight through a whiskey glass I hold
aloft sufficient wonder to remind
me of how rich I am with such fool's gold.

A Spring Birthday

March again, your month, and we watch a migrant tern
drop from the sky onto the pier's thin wall
between last year's departure and next year's return.

Courtyard in Rain, Kilmainham

It all but dances under the downpour's drum-taps,
this gravel surface
                    awash with quick-forming puddles
that will not be still,
                    the sundial's propped blade
cascading droplets, shadowless, reading hour zero.

Autumn, the Nightwalk, the City, the River

How early the autumn seemed to have come that year,
the drizzles like moods, the tightness in the air.
Walking was different: nervous, brisker now
under the streetlights' tangerine conic glow;
needing gloves and scarves. I had both,
and a raincoat pulled up tight around my mouth.
Direction never mattered on those streets.
Once I walked all night and called it quits
somewhere miles from home, then caught the first
bus back. What mattered was being lost.
Anywhere would do: I remember suburbs
plush with hatchbacks parked on tidy kerbs,
privets, cherry blossoms, *nouveaux riches'*
houses named for saints, complete with cable dishes;
and then the streets where every window was
an iron grid across its pane of glass,
the garden weeds in cracks, a noise ahead —
a bird, a cat — enough to make me cross the road.
Any light was harsh: all-night Spars
and the lit façades of Georgian squares
I'd hurry past; headlights glared like search-
beams in their hurtling, quizzical approach.
But landmarks were always a magnet. I'd be out
for hours — in sight of open fields — and spot
a pub or spire I knew, then find myself
being led by it, with inarticulate relief,
back in. Home was defeat but consolation too,
reassurance there was nowhere else to go.
The clubs all shut, town was deserted all over:
the only living thing would be the river;
and one night following it, I got a sense
of how, if anything did, it left the dead-ends
of the place behind, moving like a dream
as past barracks, churches, courts, the lot, it swam,

the lights reflected on its surface so many jack-
o'-lanterns promising no going back,
for it at least if not for me. I followed it
all the way to the quay-end and then sat
as long as I thought it would take to reach the last buoy
and from there, already forgetting dry land, open sea.

Acknowledgements and Notes

Grateful acknowledgement is made to the editors of the following publications in which these poems first appeared: *Agenda, Atlanta Review, The Big Spoon, Cobweb, College Green, Dnevi poezije in vina / Days of Poetry and Wine* (Medana, 1997), *Fortnight, Hermathena, Honest Ulsterman, The Independent, The Irish Review, The Irish Times, Lines Review, Oxford Poetry, P.N. Review, Poetry Ireland Review, Poetry Review, Quadrant, Religion and Literature, The Sunday Tribune,* and (especially) *Thumbscrew.*

'A Skimming Stone, Lough Bray' first appeared as a Turret poetry broadsheet. 'Autumn, the Nightwalk, the City, the River', was the winning poem in the 1994 Friends Provident National Poetry Competition. Thanks are also due to An Chomhairle Ealaíon/The Arts Council, Ireland, for the provision of a generous grant.

pages 56-57   'Seven from Chamfort: These versions derive
               from maxims copied but not translated by
               Samuel Beckett and preserved as MM 2929 in
               the Archive of Reading University Library,
               whose assistance I hereby gratefully acknow-
               ledge.

pages 65-71   'Thirst': Ned Kelley, not to be confused with
               his Australian namesake, was a sixteenth-
               century alchemist of Irish extraction at the
               court of Rudolf II in Prague (cf Angelo Maria
               Ripellino, *Magic Prague*, London, 1994).